BETSY HEARNE

SEVEN DISCARD BRAVE WOMEN

ILLUSTRATED BY

BETHANNE ANDERSEN

GREENWILLOW BOOKS · NEW YORK

Oil paints on a gesso background were used to create the full-color art.
The text type is Palatino.
Seven Brave Women
Text copyright © 1997 by Betsy Hearne
Illustrations copyright © 1997 by Bethanne Andersen
Manufactured in China.

Library of Congress Cataloging-in-Publication Data
Hearne, Betsy Gould.
Seven brave women / by Betsy Hearne ;
pictures by Bethanne Andersen.
p.   cm.
Summary: A young girl recounts the brave exploits of
her female ancestors, including her great-great-great-
grandmother who came to America in a wooden sailboat.
ISBN-10: 0-688-14502-7 — ISBN-10: 0-688-14503-5 (lib. bdg.) —
ISBN-10: 0-06-079921-8 (pbk.) ISBN-13: 978-0-688-14502-6 —
ISBN-13: 978-0-688-14503-3 (lib. bdg.) — ISBN-13: 978-0-06-079921-2 (pbk.)
[1. Genealogy—Fiction.   2. Courage—Fiction.]
I. Andersen, Bethanne, (date) ill.   II. Title.
PZ7.H3464Se   1997   [E]—dc20
96-10414   CIP   AC

To all the brave women,
and to their brave men, as well.

–B. H.

For Beth and Dora, who never tired of
colored pencils and messiness

–B. A.

INTRODUCTION

IN THE OLD DAYS, history books marked time by the wars that men fought. The United States began with the Revolutionary War. Then there was the War of 1812, the Civil War, the Spanish-American War, the First World War, the Second World War, the Korean War, and the Vietnam War. But there are other ways to tell time. My mother does not believe that wars should be fought at all. She says *his*tory should be *her* story, too, and she tells stories about all the women in our family who made history by not fighting in wars.

CHAPTER 1

MY GREAT-GREAT-GREAT-grandmother did great things. Elizabeth lived during the Revolutionary War, but she did not fight in it. She crossed the mountains from Switzerland, and then she crossed the sea to Philadelphia in a wooden sailboat. Her one-year-old child and her two-year-old child came with her on the boat. She was pregnant with her third baby. The food was bad. It was hard to sleep with all the babies crying. There were no bathrooms, but there were huge waves that rocked the boat back and forth, back and forth. Elizabeth was sick all the time. Sometimes she thought she would die, but she survived and had seven more children.

Elizabeth was a Mennonite. She wore plain clothes and worshiped God in strict ways. When she prayed, she knelt beside the bed and covered her head with a clean handkerchief. Every night until she died, she prayed for her husband and nine children. We still have a white handkerchief that Elizabeth embroidered with a neat, white *E*.

CHAPTER 2

MY GREAT-GREAT-GRANDMOTHER did great things. Eliza lived during the War of 1812 and the Civil War, but she did not fight in them. Instead, she moved to Ohio in a covered wagon. Her parents spoke German, but she learned English. Her parents were Mennonites, but she married a man who was not a Mennonite.

She worked on a farm all her life. Even when she was tired, or mad, or lonely, she had to work hard. She kept a herd of sheep and made blankets from their wool. We still have her spinning wheel.

She made a quilt so big it covers my bedroom wall. The stitches are so small you can hardly see them. She made candles and soap and bread and butter and jam and everything else that now you can buy at the store. She made medicine from herbs and helped her neighbors have their babies. Once, a sharp knife slipped and cut her finger open. She used the other hand to sew it up with a needle and thread.

Eliza lived to be ninety-nine years old. She grew up riding a horse and buggy, and she saw pictures of airplanes flying people through the sky before she died.

CHAPTER 3

MY GREAT-GRANDMOTHER did great things. Nellie lived during the Spanish-American War, but she did not fight in it. She worked on her mother's farm and rode her horse on a real saddle instead of the silly sidesaddles girls were supposed to use then. She loved to paint and draw, but there was no art teacher nearby. After she finished her chores on Friday morning, she rode all day to the nearest town and took art lessons from a woman who lived there. The next day, she rode all the way home in time to do Saturday's chores in the evening.

She married a preacher and planted a garden and had children and took care of her old mother (my great-great-grandmother Eliza), but she had no more time to paint pictures. Instead, she painted the china that her family ate on. We still have plates and cups and saucers and bowls—all painted with beautiful garden flowers.

CHAPTER 4

ANOTHER OF MY GREAT-GRANDMOTHERS did great things. Helen lived during World War I, but she did not fight in it. My great-grandmother was brave enough to go to medical school when it was hard for women to become doctors. Then she went to India as a missionary, but she did not save souls. She saved bodies. My great-grandmother started a hospital just for women. She delivered even more babies than my great-great-grandmother Eliza did—and also had four babies of her own. I still have the brass teapot my great-grandmother used, and the statue of a wise Indian beggar that she looked at while she drank her tea. There were many diseases among poor women she treated in the hospital, and my great-grandmother Helen died young.

CHAPTER 5

MY GRANDMOTHER DID GREAT THINGS. Betty lived during World War II, but she did not fight in it. She took fencing just for fun and played basketball on the first girls' team in her state and went to France to take harp lessons from a famous harpist there. Then she decided to be an architect. When she walked into her first class, the men met her with a sign that said: NO DOGS, CHILDREN, OR WOMEN ALLOWED. She had to take tests in a room all by herself because she was the only woman in a men's school.

My grandmother loved buildings all her life. She designed a house for her husband and children. Then she built it. She taught college students about the history of buildings. When she was eighty years old, after her husband died and her children left home and her fingers were too stiff to play the harp, she wrote a book about buildings. Everyone loved her book, so she wrote another one about builders. That book was published when she was eighty-nine years old. Taking a walk with my grandmother made you look at walls and windows in a new way. The two books she wrote still stand on our bookshelf, and her smallest harp—a green Irish lap-harp—stands on a table that belonged to her mother, my great-grandmother Nellie.

CHAPTER 6

My other grandmother did great things, too. Margaret lived during the Korean War, but she did not fight in it. From the day she was born till the day she died, she lived in the same house on Queens Boulevard in New York City. Margaret never finished high school or went to college, but she was smart. Her husband died when her two children were babies. She got a job as a secretary and took care of her sick father, her old mother, her six younger brothers and sisters, and her two children. When she was the only one left in the house on Queens Boulevard, she took in dogs and cats that had been left to starve in the street.

We don't have any of my grandmother Margaret's things, because she didn't have much herself. But we have what was most precious to her—my father.

My mother does great things.
She lived during the Vietnam War, but she did not fight in it. My mother read newspaper stories about the war, and she saw TV stories about the war. "In forests halfway across the world," she said, "the Vietnam War killed women and children who were no one's enemies. Those women and children could have been us," she said, "if we had lived there."

My mother grew up in a pine forest in Alabama. Since there was nobody else to play with, she made up stories to keep herself company. She remembered stories that she heard, and she learned stories that she read. When she grew up, she told stories to children in libraries. She told them a billion stories from all over the world—stories about Brer Rabbit, and Baba Yaga, and Babe the Blue Ox, and Balder, and Bellerophon, and banshees, and Brahmins, and Beauty and the Beast, and Bluejay, and Beowulf, and Juan Bobo, and the Baal Shem Tov. She even sang ballads. And every night, she told me stories about the brave women in our family— stories I can keep forever and pass on to my children.

CHAPTER 8

I AM NOT A WOMAN YET, but I can do great things. I can tell stories and take care of my dog and shoot basketballs and play the flute and study science and draw pictures and sew red patches on my torn jacket. I will make history the way my mother and grandmothers and great-grandmothers and great-great-grandmothers and great-great-great-grandmothers did. There are a million ways to be brave.

AUTHOR'S NOTE

THIS BOOK BEGAN with my mother's research into our family history. We know very little about the first Elizabeth except what is included in a family Bible and a few other old records. She married young, sailed on the ship *Anderson*, and eventually settled in Womelsdorf, Pennsylvania, where the stone house in which she lived and died is still standing. She bore her ninth child at the age of fifty. Her daughter, too, had a child very late in life, as did many women who survived earlier years of childbearing. About Eliza, we know a great deal more, because her daughter Nellie passed on stories to her own daughter Betty, who passed them on to me. Other branches of the family have left various tracks through time, some strong and some faint, but the pattern of these women's physical, intellectual, and spiritual strength is clear. They are, with all their human flaws, unsung heroes.